What It Means To Be
CRUCIFIED
WITH
CHRIST

Harold Vaughan

Sixth Printing
Copyright © 2003 Christ Life Publications
Printed in United States of America
ISBN 0-942889-03-7

TABLE OF CONTENTS

INTRODUCTION

Most of us have heard a great deal about the *representative* side of the Cross, which deals with the substitutionary death of Christ on Calvary. However, the average Christian is not well acquainted with the fellowship side of the Cross. The representative side deals with Christ's death for our sins. The fellowship aspect deals with our death with Christ.

The teaching of Identification is the legal side of redemption. This is the message of our union with Christ. Identification means union. Christ became what we were that we might become what He is—RIGHTEOUS!

A careful study of Scripture will reveal that Adam chose to identify himself with Satan. He actually "sided" with the Devil in unbelief and rebellion. Consequently, Adam lost his essential goodness. His union was no longer with God, but with Satan. The result—he became alive to Satan, but dead toward God.

Drastic measures had to be taken if humanity was going to be redeemed. So when Jesus went to the Cross, we went with Him. Just as "we sinned in Adam" because of our union with him, so were we crucified with Christ. This is the fellowship side of the Cross. The New Testament teaches we are crucified, dead, buried, risen, and ascended with Christ.

I suffered with Christ.
I died with Christ.
I was buried with Christ.
I was made alive with Christ.
Now I am seated with Him.

Christ became one with us in sin, that we might become one with Him in righteousness. He became one with us in death, that we might be one with Him in life. Not only was Jesus crucified *for* us, He was also crucified *as* us. Therefore, we were crucified with Him. This is the vital teaching of Identification.

This booklet is written for those who desire a fuller understanding of *What it Means To Be Crucified With Christ*. It is my prayer that the Holy Spirit would illumine your mind with the fellowship aspect of Calvary.

Harold Vaughan

Prologue
A SERPENT ON A TREE

The book of Genesis gives a vivid account of what went wrong with the human race. Man was created by God and for God. "In the image of God created he him" (Gen. 1:27). Man was the capstone of God's creation. He was given the dominion (authority) over the earth and all that pertained to it. This original man had no flaws, physical or moral. He was good in every sense of the word. Adam and Eve enjoyed fellowship with Holy God, because their nature corresponded to His (made in God's image).

Unhappily, this honeymoon came to an abrupt end as a serpent came on the scene. "Now the serpent was more subtle than any beast" (Gen. 3:1). Next to man, the serpent was the keenest and most beautiful creature. Evidently, the serpent lent itself to Satan—the first "angel of light." The serpent came to Eve, employing an indirect approach to get to the head, Adam. The rebellious snake began to strike out against God by casting doubt on His Word. "Hath God said," was the manifestation of revolt and unbelief. Then the serpent's strategy became more direct as he called God a liar! "Ye shall not surely die" (Gen. 3:4). The climax of this episode was the Fall. Man misused his freedom and joined the fallen ranks of the rebel, Satan.

It was at this point that everything changed. Man lost his dominion over the earth. A curse came upon the created world. Sin, death, suffering, and sickness resulted. Far from the paradise of the garden, man was banished from the presence of Holy God.

Man's nature no longer corresponded to God's nature. He lost his moral likeness to God and inherited the nature of the serpent, Satan! The condemned serpent-nature was immediately seen. Much like a snake, Adam and Eve were afraid of exposure, so they crouched among the trees of the garden. When they heard God walking in the garden, they hid themselves. Isn't it like a snake to hide out and seek to remain undetected? So the original couple tried to cover up and passed this evasive tendency to the lot of us. No longer were they free to be open and transparent, they were now self-conscious rather than God-conscious. Without question, they sought to be evasive with one another as well. The fig leaves outwardly corresponded to the fig leaves that shackled the inner man. This disposition of self-centeredness and isolation was demonstrated in the first two offspring of the family. Cain rose up and killed his brother. The serpentine tendency of striking out and striking back was also transmitted at the Fall.

The Fatherhood of man was transferred from God to Satan. Now man became likened in essence to his new father, the Devil. The serpent-like qualities of Satan are now resident within the being of man's fallen nature. A curse was pronounced by God on the serpent for his cooperation with Satan and a curse placed on man for his yielding to the beguiling serpent!

The ground was cursed for Adam's sake, and the snake was sentenced to crawl on his belly and eat the dust of the cursed ground. Satan had infiltrated the human family and became the prince of the world.

A second significant mention of the serpent is found in Numbers (Num. 21:9). The Israelites spoke against God and against Moses. Consequently, the Lord sent fiery serpents among the people. Many were bitten and many died. God instructed Moses to make a fiery serpent and set it upon a pole. Moses constructed a brazen serpent and erected it upon a pole. If anyone was bitten and beheld the serpent, he lived. Hearing about the snake on the pole did no good. A man needed to BEHOLD the situation for himself.

What is this other than a preview and prophecy of Jesus! The serpent is established as a symbol of sin. The serpent on the pole is symbolic of sin judged. "Look and live, look to Jesus now and live." Here we have the heart of the Gospel— sin was judged on Calvary.

"And when they were come to the place called Calvary, there they crucified him." God's Son was hanged on a cross. He that knew no sin became sin for us (2 Cor. 5:21). Jesus bore our serpentine natures on the tree. He became sin and God unleashed His wrath on Him. Jesus was my substitute. He did not die as the Son only; He died AS me and FOR me. The essence of purity and holiness was lifted up just as the brazen serpent on the pole. Here we have a great revelation, for it is written, "Cursed is everyone that hangeth on a tree." On the Cross, Jesus was condemned by God. Jesus became what I was so I could become what He is!

The first promise of a Redeemer is found in Genesis, "I will put enmity between thee and the woman, and between thy seed and her seed; it shall bruise thy head and thou shalt bruise his heel" (Gen. 3:15). The serpent Satan bruised and pierced the heel of Jesus with a spike on the Cross. What appeared to be a victory for the Devil turned out to be his own undoing. The "prince of this world" was judged at the Cross. Satan is a defeated foe. The Serpent's head has been crushed. Jesus took the serpent spirit to the Cross and provided a remedy for all who have been bitten. Everyone in Adam has but to look and see that serpent of Self crucified with Christ. The cure was death. The displacement of the old self-life made provision for the imparting of the Divine nature. Jesus did not rehabilitate or improve the serpent-self. He crushed his head and overthrew his dominion in the human heart. Now, all who come by the Cross of Christ may have eternal life. The old "I" has been crucified with Christ; it's no longer I, but Christ!

PART 1
THE PRINCIPLE

Jesus, I my cross have taken, All to leave and follow Thee.
Destitute, despised, forsaken, Thou from hence my all shalt be
Perish every fond ambition, All I've sought or hoped or known
Yet how rich is my condition: God and heaven are still my own.

". . . It is finished . . ." John 19:30

CHAPTER 1

THE CROSS:
OUT OF ADAM INTO CHRIST

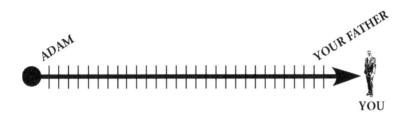

In order to comprehend the depths of the Cross it is important to understand the two Adams. The first Adam was the father of the whole human race. All of the human race is born "in Adam." In other words, we are born in the line of Adam. The diagram above illustrates this. You proceeded from your parents, who in turn proceeded from their parents. This line may be traced all the way back to Adam. If your father had died at age three, you would not be here. The reason is that you were "in" your father and your existence depended upon his. In like manner, all are born in Adam. Our existence is the consequence of Adam's existence. Therefore, we are in Adam and recipients of what he was by nature. Adam was not born a sinner, rather he was created in the image of God and had open fellowship with the Creator. Unhappily, by choice Adam disobeyed the Creator. The moment Adam sinned, he died spiritually as his fellowship with the Creator was broken. Since Adam chose to follow Satan's lie instead of God's Word, Adam became a sinner. Adam acquired a sinful nature. Consequently, all of Adam's descendants receive his sinful nature.

"For as in Adam all die" (1 Cor. 15:22). The resulting consequence of sin is death (separation from God). Because of man's inherent fallen nature, he is born into the world spiritually dead (separated from God). "Wherefore, as by one man sin entered into the world, and death by sin; and so death passed upon all men, for that all have sinned" (Rom. 5:12). The punishment for sin is death, and the only redemptive intervention is provided by Christ.

The last Adam, "Christ" (1 Cor. 15:45), took the first Adam to the Cross. The contaminated nature in Adam, and all in man that is contrary to God, was crucified with Christ. Therefore, eternal life is available to the man who will avail himself of Christ's finished work on the Cross. To be in Adam is death. To be in Christ is life. Man moves out of Adam into Christ by coming to the Cross and identifying with Christ in His death, burial, and resurrection.

Every man by nature is like the first Adam, and like the devil, for the devil and the first fallen Adam were like one another. "Ye are of *your* father the devil" (John 8:44). All the children of the first Adam are the devil's children. And all the children of the other sort are like Jesus Christ, the last Adam; and when His image shall be perfected in them, then they shall be perfectly happy. "And as we have borne the image of the earthly, we shall also bear the image of the heavenly" (1 Cor. 15:49).[1]

Christ bore our sin in His own body on the tree (1 Pet. 2:24). The last Adam was provided as an alternative for each person born into the human family. His death on the Cross provided deliverance from the penalty, power, and ultimately, the presence of sin. He accomplished this by crucifying (putting to death) the acquired fallen nature. Now it is possible to move out of Adam into Christ. Praise God for the marvelous redemption procured at Calvary!

[1] Trail, Robert: Holiness, J.C. Ryle, page 461.

Out of Adam into Christ

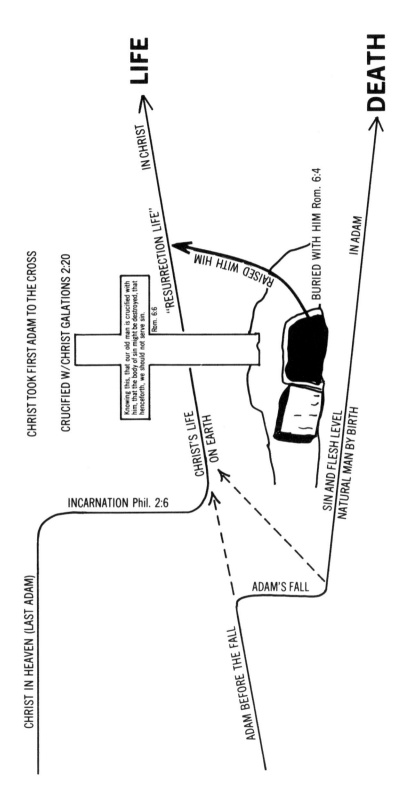

LIFE

DEATH

CHRIST TOOK FIRST ADAM TO THE CROSS

CRUCIFIED W/CHRIST GALATIONS 2:20

Knowing this, that our old man is crucified with him, that the body of sin might be destroyed, that henceforth, we should not serve sin.
Rom. 6:6

IN CHRIST

"RESURRECTION LIFE"

RAISED WITH HIM

BURIED WITH HIM Rom. 6:4

IN ADAM

CHRIST'S LIFE ON EARTH

SIN AND FLESH LEVEL
NATURAL MAN BY BIRTH

INCARNATION Phil. 2:6

CHRIST IN HEAVEN (LAST ADAM)

ADAM'S FALL

ADAM BEFORE THE FALL

CHAPTER 2

THE CROSS:
THE STOPPING PLACE FOR SIN

"For he hath made him to be sin" (2 Corinthians 5:21).

The Cross of Christ is the place where God once and forever settled the sin problem. The combined sins of the human race were nailed to that tree "in His own body." The composite transgressions of Adam's race were inflicted on Christ. He who was sinless became the very essence of sin. The wrath of God against sin was unleashed in full force at Calvary! In one sense, sin is not forgiven; it must be judged. Jesus took the punishment in our place as His atoning blood was shed for the sins of the world. The Almighty heaped all the sin of all time upon Christ on the Cross. This sacrifice settled forever the problem of sin to God's complete satisfaction. The blood of Christ was sufficient for God.

"For as in Adam all die, even so in Christ shall all be made alive" (1 Cor. 15:22). The fallen nature is transmitted through birth. At conception, an individual receives a carnal nature that is at enmity with God. This old Adamic nature is the root of sin. To redeem us from the curse of sin, the Lord Jesus had to deal with the source. So total was Adam's Fall that the only deliverance was death. The last Adam took the first Adam to the Cross. "Knowing this, that our old man is crucified with him..." (Rom. 6:6). Before a man can be born from above, he must die. Galatians 2:20 in literal rendering explains it completely: "I have been crucified with Christ." The Adamic nature was crucified with Christ, resulting in a death blow to the source of sin.

The Cross is the stopping place for sin. Believers must do with sin the same as God did with it. We must put our sins on the Cross and leave them there. By accepting Christ as Saviour, we moved out of Adam into Christ. The Cross is where God dealt with sin. The atoning blood of Christ took away our sins. He was made sin "that we might be made the righteousness of God in him." Our sins became His; His righteousness became ours.

To illustrate: Suppose you had a bow and arrow, but the end of the arrow was covered with a ball of wax about the size of an orange. You pull the bowstring back and shoot the arrow. The arrow hits the bull's eye on the target. The arrow penetrates the target; it goes through the wax all the way out the other side of the target. However, the wax at the moment of impact, splattered all across the bull's eye. The wax stayed on the near side of the target while the arrow came out the far side. At Calvary, our old nature and sin were stopped. It was put to death (rendered inoperative). Nevertheless, we went through Calvary with Christ and came out on the resurrection side. Like a polished shaft, we have come through the cross to walk in newness of life. Sin and self were dealt a death blow, but Jesus rose again! The cross was the stopping place for sin, just as the target was the stopping place for the wax. The arrow kept on going through both the wax and the target. In like manner, Jesus kept on going through Calvary. He did not stop there! He rose again! Forgiveness and deliverance from the power of sin is available because of Calvary. The cross is truly the stopping place for sin.

CHAPTER 3

THE CROSS: THE BELIEVER'S IDENTIFICATION WITH CHRIST

"Because we thus judge, that if one died for all, then were all dead" (2 Corinthians 5:14).

Christ had to be willing to identify Himself with us in order to redeem us. Since the human race was ruined by a man, it had to be redeemed by a man. Mankind suffered wreckage and downfall through Adam's transgression. Before Christ could reclaim humanity, He had to be willing to stand in the place of humanity. "Forasmuch then as the children are partakers of flesh and blood, he also himself likewise took part of the same ... For verily he took not on him the nature of angels; but he took on him the seed of Abraham. Wherefore in all things it behooved him to be made like unto his brethren ...to make reconciliation for the sins of the people" (Heb. 2:14-17).

Christ willingly humbled Himself and empathized with man. "...[He] was in all points tempted like as we are, yet without sin" (Heb. 4:15). Through the representative Man (Adam) the human family fell. Through the representative Man (Christ) the human family was redeemed.

"[Jesus] made himself of no reputation, and took upon him the form of a servant, and was made in the likeness of men: And being found in fashion as a man, he humbled himself, and became obedient unto death..." (Phil. 2:7-8). Christ was born of a virgin and took on a human frame, laying aside His reputation. Since salvation was only possible through a broken Saviour, Jesus experienced a broken will at Gethsemane, a broken body on the Cross, a broken fellowship with the Father at Calvary. Brokenness epitomized Jesus in His identification with us as He provided our redemption.

As Christ identified with us, we must be willing to identify with Him. Man also has to be broken. The self-centered sinner must break at the foot of the Cross. "The sacrifices of God are a broken spirit and a contrite heart," says the Bible. Jesus was broken on the Cross and we must be broken at the Cross. The walls of pride, self-righteousness, and respectability must come crashing down before rivers of living water can come forth. Just as He laid aside his reputation, so must we identify with Christ in His death, burial, and resurrection. Present-day Americans did not write the Constitution or forge out the freedoms that they presently enjoy. However, we today are identified with our forefathers who secured that liberty. In like manner, the Christian is identified with Christ. He did the work on our behalf. Our part is to accept our co-crucifixion with Christ as a fact and act on it by faith. Since we were crucified with Christ, we were also buried and raised to walk in newness of life with Him. We are no longer children of the Devil. On the contrary, we have a new identity as children of God by virtue of our identification with Christ. Not only have we been crucified, buried, and raised with Christ, but we have also ascended with Christ positionally. "Even when we were dead in sins, hath (He) quickened us together with Christ...And hath raised us up together, and made us sit together in heavenly places in Christ Jesus" (Eph. 2:5-6). The believer's new identity is "union with Christ" in the spiritual sphere.

CHAPTER 4

THE CROSS:
THE ROOT OF THE MATTER

The Cross of Christ has dealt with the deepest need of man, the need to restore his complete fellowship with God. Since sin hinders this restored fellowship with God, Christ's death on the Cross provided more than a mere cosmetic cover-up for man's need. The Cross dealt with the source of sin, not just the symptom of the sin itself. Romans 5:21 states, "That as sin hath reigned unto death, even so might grace reign through righteousness unto eternal life by Jesus Christ our Lord."

Sins are the product of the sin nature. Adam's fall into sin put a curse upon the whole human race. "Wherefore, as by one man sin entered into the world..." states Romans 5:12. Consequently, "...by one man's disobedience many were made sinners" (Rom. 5:19). The natural thing for a sinner to do is sin! His sins are the result of what he is, a sinner. It is not enough just to deal with sins, which are symptomatic. God went beyond man's sins and dealt directly with the source of sin—the fallen satanic nature. The term *self-life* will be subsequently used in this work to describe the sin nature. The self-life includes all in man that is contrary to God and is the root problem to restoring complete fellowship of man with God. The following diagram illustrates the progression of the self-life to its outward manifestations.

OUTWARD SINS

HEART SINS

PRIDE   LUST

SELF-LIFE

Issuing forth from the base of the self-life, lust and pride extend the ascendancy of sin to the second level. "For all that is in the world, the lust of the flesh, and the lust of the eyes, and the pride of life, is not of the Father..." (1 Jn. 2:16). Lust and pride stem from the root of the self-life and are the basic avenues in which the self-life expresses itself. The lust of the flesh can be viewed as the desire *to experience* (sensuality); the lust of the eyes as the desire *to possess* (coveteousness); and the pride of life as the desire *to be* (pride)—the desire to be number one!

The third level of sins issuing from the self-life are the sins of the heart. Heart sins stem from the second level of lust and pride. "For from within, out of the heart of men, proceed evil thoughts, adulteries, fornication...All these evil things come from within..." (Mk. 7:21-23). Heart sins are inner sins. They have to do with attitudes and motives, such as hatred, bitterness, resentment, jealousy, apathy, and lukewarmness. These are inner sins and have not yet reached the surface of outward expression.

Proceeding out of the heart sins is the fourth level called

outward sins. The outward sins are the visible expression of the self-life. They have to do with the apparent actions of the flesh such as drinking, lying, gossip, unfriendliness, and adultery. These are overt expressions of the fallen nature and can be traced back to the source of the self-life.

The self-life produced in Adam at the Fall was beyond salvage. The only cure for it was death. This is precisely what happened at Calvary. The Lord Jesus was able to save man from sin by taking the culprit of self in His body to the Cross. "I am crucified with Christ" (Gal. 2:20). Positionally and judicially, the self-life has been put out of commission by the Cross.

In Romans 6:6 the "old man" is translated "self" (Weymouth, Williams, and Amplified Translations). As previously mentioned, the self-life expresses a contaminated, proud, selfish nature that prevents the reality of the "Christlife" in the personality of the believer. Being "crucified with Christ" and talking about death does not mean personality is destroyed. The death aspect deals only with the old self that distorts and destroys God's fulfillment in life. The Cross does not destroy the individual's essential personality. Rather it releases the person from the bondage of sin and cancels Satan's authority over him. The believer with his purified personality is meet for the Master's use.

Now that the self-life has been dealt with by death (crucified with Christ), the believer receives a new nature (2 Pet. 1:4). The *old man* is replaced by the *new man* "...which is Christ in you, the hope of glory" (Col. 1:27). Our identification with Christ in His death remedied our fallen state and we are saved by His life within us. "...We were reconciled to God by the death of his son, much more...we shall be saved by his life" (Rom. 5:10).

OUTWARD SINS

HEART SINS

PRIDE
and
LUST

Fruit - Outward Sins
Branches - Heart Sins
Trunk - Pride and Lust
Root - Self Life

SELF LIFE

CHAPTER 5

THE CROSS: WE DIED WITH HIM

"If we be dead with him, we shall also live with him"
(2 Timothy 2:11).

When Paul speaks of death with Christ he speaks of a past occurrence. The Greek scholar, Kenneth Wuest, renders the above passage, "in view of the fact that we died with Him." What type of death does this refer to? Obviously, it cannot be referring to physical death. It refers to spiritual death.

In the mind of the Almighty, we died to sin and its dominion when we died with Christ. "For he that is dead is freed from sin" (Rom. 6:7). There was in God's mind at the crucifixion a perfect oneness of Christ with us. "Who his own self bare our sins in his own body on the tree, that we, being dead to sins…"(1 Pet. 2:24). He partook of our spiritual death. We were utterly one with Him in that Judgment. His death and our death are identical.

This union is further emphasized in Colossians 3:3, "For ye are dead, and your life is hid with Christ in God." We were one with Him on the Cross. We were one with Him in His death. This union was complete. It had to be, because our union with Satan (sin) was a perfect union. By natural birth mankind is one in alliance with the Devil.

Here is the strategy of Calvary: "For he hath made him to be sin for us, who knew no sin; that we might be made the righteousness of God in him" (2 Cor. 5:21). He drank the cup of death that we might drink the cup of life. He became one with us in weakness, in sin, and in spiritual death, that He might make us one with Himself in righteousness and fellowship with the Father. He became death's prisoner in order to set us free!

"Wherefore if ye be dead with Christ…" (Col. 2:20) is another text teaching the same truth. In Christ we died to the dominion of Satan, sin, the world, habits, and circumstances.

Because Jesus bore our spiritual death we need not die again. Rather, He has called us to live and reign with Him. His perfect redemption is ours. His perfect righteousness is ours. "And ye are complete in him…" (Col. 2:10). All He is and did is ours. All we are is His. Jesus' prayer "that they all may be one" was fulfilled when the Father made us one with Himself in Christ.

CHAPTER 6

THE CROSS: THE BELIEVER'S ROAD TO VICTORY

Apprehending the Cross in principle and experience is the road to deliverance. While much is said today about Christ's death for sin, very little is said about death to sin. The Cross stands paramount in history as the greatest "unshackling" event ever. Let us look at the fourfold deliverance secured at the Cross.

1. Sins. "For I delivered unto you first of all...how that Christ died for our sins..." (1 Cor. 15:3). The justice of God required punishment for man's sin before His forgiveness of man was possible. The punishment for all mankind's sin was accomplished in the person of Christ. He shed His blood on the Cross, thereby satisfying God's requirement for a blood sacrifice. "In whom we have redemption through his blood, the forgiveness of sins..." (Eph. 1:7). Forgiveness for sins is possible because Christ "bare our sins in his own body on the tree..." (1 Peter 2:24). The death of Christ has forever settled the penalty for sins. "As far as the east is from the west, so far hath he removed our transgressions from us" (Ps. 103:12).

2. Flesh. "And they who belong to Christ Jesus crucified the flesh (evil nature) with its dispositions and cravings once for all" (Gal. 5:24, Wuest Expanded Translation). The word **flesh** here refers to the fallen nature of those born in Adam. The flesh is the root from which the fruit of sins springs forth. In other words, sins are the product of the principle of sin resident in man at his birth. "And they going astray became flesh" (Gen. 6:3, Conybeare). The Cross not only secured forgiveness for sins, but also conquered the flesh by crucifying it. Death on the Cross is the pathway to life. "Knowing this experientially, that our old (unregenerate) self was crucified once for all with Him in order that the physical body (heretofore) dominated by the sinful nature might be rendered inoperative (in that respect), with the result that no longer are we rendering a slave's habitual obedience to the sinful nature, for the one who died once for all stands in the position of a permanent relationship of freedom from the sinful nature" (Rom. 6:6-7, Wuest Expanded Translation).

The power of the flesh was broken at the Cross. Hence, the believer is no longer obligated to sin, "For he that is dead is freed from sin" (Rom. 6:7).

3. World. "But God forbid that I should glory, save in the cross of our Lord Jesus Christ, by whom the world is crucified unto me, and I unto the world" (Gal. 6:14). In this passage of Scripture the word **world** refers to the world system or evil age. The present age lies under the domain of the Prince of the power of the air, or Satan. The world system is dominated by the "…spirit that now worketh in the children of disobedience" (Eph. 2:2). Hence, the world system is under a curse resulting from Adam's fall in the garden. This world spirit lies in opposition to God's Holy Spirit.

The world and all God originally created was beautiful, perfect, and good. However, the entrance of sin has produced an abnormal world system which is satanic in nature because it opposes God's authority. The dust of death lies upon this present age.

The good news is that the believer is released from the world spirit by means of crucifixion with Christ. The dominance of the world's hold was broken at the Cross. The world spirit is no longer dominant within the believer's life, and the world system is no longer the rule of his life without. The Holy Spirit resides in the human spirit and displaces the world.

4. Satan. "And having spoiled principalities and powers, he made a show of them openly, triumphing over them in it" (Col. 2:15). Adam's descendants are born children of the Evil One. However, Calvary has provided the means whereby the sinner becomes the saint. Satan is a defeated foe because his power over the redeemed has been canceled. "Who hath delivered us from the power of darkness, and hath translated us into the kingdom of his dear Son" (Col. 1:13). Those at enmity with God have become the friends of God by adoption. The believer is therefore freed from the control, the nature, and the power of Satan. He and his host of demonic spirits are now subject to the name of Jesus.

"If the Son therefore shall make you free, ye shall be free indeed" (Jn. 8:36). Christ has overcome everything that is contrary to the Christian; sins, flesh, the world, and Satan were conquered on the Cross. Hence, the Cross is the believer's road to victory.

PART 2
THE REALITY

Dying with Jesus, His death reckoned mine,
Living with Jesus, a new life divine
Looking to Jesus till glory doth shine
Moment by moment, oh Lord, I am thine.

". . . Christ liveth in me . . ." Galatians 2:20

CHAPTER 7

THE CROSS:
CALVARY PRECEDES PENTECOST

"...work out your own salvation...For it is God which worketh in you..."(Philippians 2:12-13).

Calvary must be a finality before Pentecost can become a reality! If self is not dealt with, then the believer's life will be an endless treadmill of sinning, repenting, and confessing. The application of the Cross to the self-life is the only means of deliverance. The self-life must be consigned to the Cross so the Spirit can reign. Jesus can be seen only when the big "I" has been removed.

There must be a working out of what God has worked in. "It is God which worketh in you." First, God works in us, then He tells us to "work out" that which He has worked in. Nowhere is this more true than with the Cross. By design, God works the Cross into the living level of life for His children. His working in us is contingent upon our outward working. Normally, this is a gradual process whereby the believer is stripped of self-will, self-effort, and self-glory. God seeks our cooperation through proper response to our circumstances. Though the Cross is complete in principle, nevertheless, there is a practical outworking in the individual life.

Unhappily, much of modern preaching circumvents the Cross. Slowly but surely, the true meaning of Calvary has been all but lost. In Jesus' day if a man had taken up his cross, it meant the end. He had already said goodbye to his family and friends. He knew he would not be coming back! The cross meant death. However, a new cross is being preached today. It uses the same words and symbolically embraces the same theology as the old. This new cross does not demand the end of the man or his independence. It merely redirects the man and gives him life, only on a higher religious plane. This new, smooth cross stands in contrast to the old rugged Cross of Scripture. The acceptance of Christ as Lord no longer necessitates repentance or departure from sin. Receiving Christ is seen to be only another step on the worldling's way to the top! Promises of success, prosperity, and ecstasy are offered to those who would respond. People walk down aisles blowing bubbles and telling jokes as they commit their lives to Christ.

The problem with this is that it bypasses the Cross. Surely, God wants us to walk in resurrection power. But Calvary precedes Pentecost—both in history and in experience. "...Except a corn of wheat fall into the ground and die, it abideth alone: but if it die, it bringeth forth much fruit" (John 12:24).

.

CHAPTER 8

THE CROSS:
THE WAY OF DEATH

"...If any man will come after me, let him deny himself, and take up his cross daily, and follow me" (Luke 9:23).

On New Year's Day in 1863, Abraham Lincoln spent hours poring over one of the most important documents in the history of America, the Emancipation Proclamation. When signed, this document would set every slave in America free. Lincoln signed the important document that day. However, in those days word traveled slowly, and in Texas some slaves did not hear of the Emancipation Proclamation until June 19 that same year. The slaves were legally freed on New Year's Day, but they lived without knowledge of the freedom they had gained. Many slaves, even after they had heard of their freedom, did not accept it. They had been slaves all their lives and did not know where to go, what to do, or how to function independently. Many slaves were positionally free, but practically bound. Legally, they were free, yet many were still dominated by their cruel, ruthless masters. Some slavemasters even refused to let them go. Likewise, the Cross of the Lord Jesus Christ is the Christian's emancipating proclamation. All Christians have been legally and positionally set free from the old cruel, ruthless master of sin, but practically they are still bound. By applying the Cross of Christ, we can be free from the old power that has mastered us.

The Lord Jesus invited all who follow Him to take up the cross. In essence He said, "I am going to the cross. I am going to die. If you want to follow Me, you must follow Me to Calvary *daily*." This daily application of the Cross has been expressed as taking a faith stand on Calvary. This is not a passive submission but an active stand by faith. Once a pastor from America was visiting the Holy Land. When his group came to Calvary the tour guide asked the pastor if he had been there before. The pastor said, "Yes, I was here about two thousand years ago when I was crucified with Christ." It is a daily banking upon the provision Christ made on the Cross.

There is much confusion at this point. Satan has bewildered the church with all sorts of extremes. It is not my purpose to discuss the multitude of views. Rather, I think it is important to realize that sin is a *choice*. Before salvation a person has no choice; all he can do is sin. "In the flesh" he cannot know, please, or obey God. Since he has bad *blood,* spiritually he is bound to sin. However, after salvation everything is reversed. The believer no longer *has* to sin; he has to choose to sin. His new nature enables him to know, obey, and please God. Sin was normal before salvation but is now abnormal. "...How shall we, that are dead to sin, live any longer therein?" (Rom. 6:2). Believers are no longer bound to sin. In fact, when a Christian sins it is because he chooses to. It is by an active choice of his will.

The Cross renders inoperative the principle of sin. To "take up the cross daily" is to acknowledge by faith our crucifixion with Christ. It is choosing to gaze at our *position* rather than our *condition*. Many Christians view themselves as victims instead of victors. They have not learned to consider the power of the Cross.

"For sin shall not have dominion over you..." (Rom. 6:14). The power of the old slavemaster, sin, was broken at

Calvary. Romans 6 tells us that we died unto sin with Christ. "...We have been planted together in the likeness of his death..." (Rom. 6:5). When you visualize Calvary in your mind, begin to see your old life crucified with Christ. The corruption of the serpent nature was crucified. By accounting this to be true the believer learns to take a faith stand and walk by faith. This is the daily application of the Cross. This is learning not to live on see-level but heaven's level.

Let me illustrate the point by using the following parable. Fact, Faith and Feeling are walking on a narrow ledge. Fact is leading the way. Faith is following Fact. Feeling is behind Faith. Fact moves steadily along with no problems at all. Faith does fine as long as he looks directly at Fact. But Faith momentarily takes his eyes off of Fact and briefly glances at Feeling. Instantaneously, Faith and Feeling tumble off the ledge. They brush themselves off and stand looking around at one another. Fact is doing just fine and is still right on course. Faith and Feeling remain in the pit until Faith chooses to fix his eyes on Fact. Immediately, when Faith gazes at Fact, both Faith and Feeling are back up on the ledge and doing just fine. This is learning to live life in the proper order and with the proper perspective.

In order to take up the cross daily we must observe three things:

Fact: "I have been crucified with Christ." Christ's death was our death to sin. His resurrection was our resurrection to life. Christ is now our life. Legally and positionally, we are free.

Faith: By faith we must account the Fact to be true. "Likewise *reckon* ye also yourselves to be dead indeed unto sin..." (Rom 6:11). We do not reckon in order to become dead, we reckon because we are dead to sin. Our faith focus must be held on Fact. We dare not continually gaze at circumstance or Feeling. Daily we must appropriate the liberating power of the Cross. It is our legal right to freedom and we must enforce our emancipation by appropriating the authority of the Cross to cancel the power of sin.

Filling: The filling of the Holy Spirit pertains to the resurrection side of the Cross. Holy Spirit-control is possible only because Calvary breaks the power of sin-control. The Bible teaches that those who have been immersed into death with Christ have also been raised to walk in newness of life (Rom. 6:3, 4). This "newness of life" is life in the Spirit. The Lord Jesus has given us His Holy Spirit to dwell in us and lead us.

How are we filled with the Holy Spirit? Believing God, we confess our sins for cleansing, and reckon ourselves dead to sin for deliverance, and ask for the filling of the Holy Spirit for victory. This is a daily process of the emptying out of sin, reckoning, and receiving the filling of the Holy Spirit.

CHAPTER 9

THE CROSS:
THE ALTAR FOR SELF

"Knowing this, that our old man is crucified with him..."
(Romans 6:6).

According to Judges 3, the nation of Israel was in bondage to an alien king. The Israelites were forced to pay tribute to King Eglon. This powerful ruler forced his will on the people as a slavemaster would upon a slave. There arose a deliverer named Ehud, who dealt directly with the problem. He could have raised up an army of rebels to fight the enemy's soldiers. Rather, he went straight to the source of the problem, which was the wrong man on the throne. He secured deliverance for the nation of Israel by eliminating the (wrong) man who occupied the throne.

This Old Testament account precisely illustrates man's basic problem—the wrong man on the throne. The big **"I"** is in control instead of Jesus. To render the carnal nature inoperative, it is essential to understand the work of Calvary. Jesus displaced the "old man" from the throne by taking him to the Cross.

1. Principle of Knowledge. Knowledge is a necessary element in the intellectual comprehension of what happened to our self-life on Calvary. A co-crucifixion took place on Christ's Cross. "And they that are Christ's have crucified the flesh with the affections and lusts" (Gal. 5:24). The flesh, or the carnal nature, was judicially crucified with Christ; therefore, it was ended, not mended. Knowing the fact precedes practical benefit. The truth we *know* sets us free. God has so designed us that truth feeds through the mind before we can act on it. Before salvation you heard that Christ died for you on the Cross. Your decision to become a Christian was based on that fact. Therefore, you chose to take advantage of what Christ did, accepting Him into your life. So it is with this truth. You must hear it and accept it by faith just as you received Christ. "Knowing that our old man has been crucified." This is something which has already taken place. You were crucified with Christ.

L. E. Maxwell illustrates with the following story from his book *Born Crucified*. During the Civil War, George Wyatt was chosen by lot to go to the front lines. Since he had a wife and six children, a young man named Richard Pratt offered to go in his place. Pratt was accepted and joined the ranks bearing the name and number of George Wyatt. Soon Pratt was killed in action. Sometime later, Wyatt was again drafted into military service. He protested, entering the plea that he had died in the person of Pratt. He insisted that the authorities consult their own records as to the fact of his having died in identification with Pratt. It was acknowledged that he had died in the person of his substitute. He was thereby exempted from further service for he had died in the person of his representative.

In the spiritual realm, Christ was your substitute. You died in identification with Him as your representative.

2. Principle of Faith. "The just shall live by faith." The victorious Christian life is a life of dependence upon God and His Word. "Without faith it is impossible to please God."

It is not enough just to know truth. Truth must be appropriated by faith. Faith is more than mental assent to certain facts. It is believing God to work the truth into your daily life.

"…Reckon ye also yourselves to be dead indeed unto

sin…" (Rom. 6:11). It is a fact that you have died unto sin "with Christ." You must account that to be true in your life. You must agree with God. This is not self-crucifixion, for it is impossible for a man to crucify himself physically. He could nail his feet and one hand to the cross, but the other hand would remain free. Likewise, we need not attempt to crucify ourselves or "die to self." By faith you must "reckon" (account it to be so) self dead with Christ. You do not reckon *in order to become* dead to sin, you reckon because you *are!* Take God at His Word. Incidentally, this has absolutely nothing to do with feelings. Faith is not determined by emotion, but is an act of the will that chooses to believe God. The life of faith is a foreign sphere to the natural man because he walks by sight and not by faith.

3. The Principle of Time. "He must increase, but I must decrease" (John 3:30). The Christian life is a maturing process. As the self-life diminishes in conformity to His death (Phil. 3:10), the life of the Lord Jesus becomes increasingly dominant! God has started a good work in you; He intends to finish it.

The Holy Spirit applies the truth as it is activated by faith and works it out in the experience of the believer. It is an ever-deepening process. The revelation to the mind may be instantaneous, but the grafting into the living level of life is normally gradual and progressive. A careful study of biblical giants will reveal that saints are "grown" and not "made." It took time for God to mature Moses, Abraham, and David. It will also take time for God to mature us. God knows the human race tends to learn slowly and He deals with us gently. Romans tells us we are to present our bodies a living sacrifice to God. The problem with a living sacrifice is that it keeps jumping off the altar! This problem is taken care of by the prayer in Psalm 118:27— "…bind the sacrifice with cords, even unto the horns of the altar." In Old Testament days the practice was to tie the living sacrifice with cords by the four legs to the horns of the altar. This prevented it from getting off the altar once it was placed there. We need to ask God to bind us to the altar in exactly the same way. The Holy Spirit reveals one area of the self-life at a time. As soon as it is recognized, immediately take that area to the Cross and leave it there. Gradually, the self-life will decrease its influence while the new nature will gain ground. "Growing in grace" is walking with God one step at a time.

CHAPTER 10

THE CROSS:
THE CROSS IN EXPERIENCE

"That I may know him . . . the power of his resurrection . . . the fellowship of his sufferings, being made conformable unto his death" (Phil. 3:10).

As previously mentioned, the Cross (to the Christian) is both an historical event and a contemporary experience. Everything that pertains to life and godliness is available to the saint who is growing in grace. Spiritual growth, then, is becoming what I already am in Christ! It is coming to a clearer understanding of my true position. Now, as the truth of the Cross comes into unclouded focus, the outer life is affected. This is the outer working of inner revelation. It is the ongoing process of sanctification.

A man and wife lived on a plantation. They enjoyed one another and had a wonderful, intimate marriage. After 30 years of marriage, the husband passed away. The wife was brokenhearted. She couldn't bear to part with him physically, so she had her husband embalmed, bought him some new clothes, and brought him home with her. She sat him in his favorite chair in the living room. She then had a glass box constructed and placed right over the corpse of her husband as he sat in the chair. She would come home every afternoon and speak to him. After several months, she decided to take a trip to England. Within a matter of days, she met an Englishman and fell in love. Marriage resulted and they spent their honeymoon in Europe before returning to America. She brought her new husband home to Alabama. She had forgotten to tell the new husband about the old husband sitting in the living room in her home. The Britisher picked her up, carried her across the threshold of the living room and suddenly spotted the fellow sitting in the chair. He immediately dropped her to the floor and exclaimed, "Who's that?" She replied, "Well, I forgot to tell you. That is my old husband." The new husband quickly replied, "The old man simply has to go. You're under new management now!"

"Being made conformable unto his death" is dying to the old self-dependent way of life. Gradually, the Holy Spirit will bring to light one area at a time. God deals gently with His children and chastens them to bring about conformity to His Son. This is the outworking of the Cross. Hidden sins of jealousy, pride, cowardice, self-will, self-seeking, and self-glory must be laid bare at the Cross. God seeks to bring us to the end of ourselves that we might come into the fullness of Christ. This is the Christ-life— "being made conformable unto his death."

As the Holy Spirit brings new areas to light, the sincere believer must agree with God. The Lord never lets us *down*, but He never lets us *off*, apart from our being honest with Him, ourselves, and others. Any remnants of the old life must be consigned to the Cross, where God put them on His Son. The exchanged life is appropriating His fullness to replace our emptiness. Humility instead of pride. Confidence in place of fear. Praise rather than complaining. Victory instead of defeat.

Often we think God's best gifts are on the top shelf where we have to tiptoe and strive to receive them. To the contrary, God's best gifts are on the bottom shelf right next to the ground. We have to bend our stiff necks in order to get them! "Being made conformable unto his death."

The outworking of the Cross is not to condemn us but to deliver us. We stand in need of deliverance in addition to cleansing. Suppose there was a roadway atop a mountain. The road followed the flat contour of the mountain for miles but suddenly dropped off with a severe turn to the left. There are two choices on how to deal with this situation. First, road crews could put up flashing lights, traffic bumps, guard rails, and speed limit signs. Any number of measures could be utilized to warn unsuspecting drivers of the approaching danger. This would be *preventative*. The other alternative would be to construct a hospital at the bottom of the mountain. Also, there would be a need for wreckers, ambulances, and medical personnel, for many people would inevitably run off the cliff. This would be a *corrective* measure. Most have been taught a *corrective* theology (how to clean up after you have run off the cliff)! There is a place for 1 John 1:9, but this is not the place to stop. What we need is a *preventative* theology (how not to run off the cliff in the first place). God never intended habitual defeat for His own. Appropriating our death with Christ and being made conformable to His death are God's way of teaching us to live above sin. We must remember that sin is a choice. We do not have to sin. Romans 6 is *preventative* theology!

Paul's expressed desire "to know him" means to know by experience. Paul wants to come to know Christ by experience. He wished to know the same power that raised Jesus from the dead. Also, mention is made of entering into the fellowship of His sufferings. This joint participation of Christ's sufferings is not His substitutionary sufferings, but His sufferings for righteousness' sake while on earth.

Through experiencing the resurrection power surging through his being and becoming a joint-participant in Christ's sufferings, Paul would be constantly "made conformable unto his death." The words "made conformable" mean, literally, "to bring to the same form with some other person" (Wuest). This does not refer to a physical death but a conformity to the spirit and temper of Christ's life in meekness, lowliness, and submission. The power of the Cross severs all that is unlike Jesus and cancels out the power of sin in death. "Being made conformable unto his death." The victory over sin is already won, but Christ's victory must be enforced by faith. By faith you received pardon; by faith take victory!

We believers are under new management; therefore, Scripture tells us to "walk in the Spirit." We are espoused to a new husband, even Christ. One night a man on crutches checked into a motel. One of his legs was crippled and the other healthy. He could not walk without the aid of crutches. Early in the morning he was seen in the swimming pool swimming freely back and forth. Then a strange scene occurred. In water shoulder-high he walked a straight line from one side of the pool to the other. This was repeated several times, after which he got out of the pool. Once out of the water he had to have crutches again. He was handicapped out of the pool. The buoyancy of the water held him up and allowed him to swim and walk freely. In like manner, a Christian can walk uprightly in the sphere of the Spirit. The Spirit buoys him up and he has no problem as long as he stays in the "water" of the Spirit. But if the believer moves out of the control of the Spirit he is crippled spiritually and cannot walk properly. The old life must sink into death in order for the Spirit to have sway.

CHAPTER 11

THE CROSS: PATHWAY TO LIFE

*"...Ye are circumcised with the circumcision made without hands, in putting off . . . the flesh . . . Buried with him in baptism . . . also **ye are risen with him**" (Colossians 2:11-12).*

Calvary means the end for the old life and the beginning of the new life. The circumcision heretofore mentioned is not external, but inward; not made with hands, but wrought by the Spirit. The reference is to the heart and not the physical body. The term flesh represents the whole carnal desire. Hence, spiritual circumcision is the severing and cutting away of the fleshly nature. This stripping away has been accomplished "by the circumcision of Christ." The physical circumcision removed only a part of the body. In the spiritual circumcision through Christ, the whole corrupt carnal nature is put away like a piece of clothing when removed and laid aside. The power of the self-life is broken at the Cross.

Verse 12 begins, "Buried with him in baptism." Again, this refers to the believer's union with Christ in His death, burial and resurrection. This verse echoes the concept found in Romans 6:3-4 – *Do you not know that so many of us as were placed in Jesus Christ, were introduced into his death? Therefore we were buried with Him.*

By virtue of identification with Christ in His death, the power of indwelling sin is broken. "For he that is dead is freed from sin" (Rom. 6:7). The believer's identification with Christ in His resurrection has resulted in the implantation of the divine nature. Thus, "risen with him" does not refer to our future physical resurrection, but to our spiritual resurrection from a sinful state into divine life!

The old life is ended, but the new life has just started. The co-crucifixion with Christ and death-union with Christ is not the end of the story. They merely serve as the pathway to resurrection and ascension life. Unfortunately, some seem to be stuck, having never come through to experiential life in the Spirit.

The work of the Cross is a completed task. Jesus did it all. Now the Lord waits for His children to enter in by simply appropriating the fullness of Christ by faith. "As ye have therefore received Christ Jesus the Lord, so walk ye in him: Rooted and built up in him, and stablished in the faith, as ye have been taught…" (Col. 2:6-7).

CHAPTER 12

THE CROSS:
A DIVINE GO-BETWEEN

Botanists tell us that across the leaf-stalk there forms in autumn a layer of thin-walled cells. These are termed "the layer of separation." These press and tear the older cells apart and become disintegrated in their turn, until, without an effort, the leaf detaches with a severance as clean and sharp as if made by a knife. The plant sentences the leaf to death, and the wind carries out the sentence.

But where is the barrier that we can place between ourselves and the old self-centered life? Where is the sentence of death that we can pass upon it? Back to the Cross! It is our divine "layer of separation."

There are only two kinds of people in the world: those who are "dead *in* sin" and those who are "dead *to* sin"!

There is a way of escape from the endless treadmill of sinning, confessing, and repenting, wherein many a soul beats its wings for years. The question of pardon for sin may have been settled long ago, but there is still a struggle with the power of sin. There is no other way to pass from today to tomorrow except through the night. There is no other way to pass from the old life to the new, except by passing through the Cross.

A stage of dying must come over the plant before the new leaves can grow and thrive. There is a deliberate choice between the former growth and the new growth. The twig must withdraw its sap from last year's leaf, and let it flow into this year's bud.

The Cross of Christ shuts off the life of sin. Like the

layer of separation, it stands as a barrier between us and the power of sin, as we "reckon" it there—that is, hold it there by faith.

The will (the sap) is withdrawn from the former existence, aims and desires, and is sent into the new. It is given over to the other side. We hold to it that we have passed from death to life through the Cross with Christ. Christ is now our life. We reckon ourselves dead to the old; we reckon ourselves alive in the new by faith. Reckoning does not stop at death, but goes on to life. Spiritual growth means more than sweeping away the leaves of sin—it means the Lord Jesus developed in us.

But is it an act or a gradual process? It is a resolve *taken once for all* on the basis of Calvary and it is carried out in detail day by day. From the first hour that the layer of separation began to form in the leaf-stalk, the leaf's fate is sealed; there is never a moment's reversal of the decision and process.

Each day that follows is a steady carrying out of the plant's purpose: "The old leaf shall die, and the new leaf shall live." Put the Cross of Christ and its power irrevocably between you and the source of sin, and hold it there in the rest of faith. That is your part, and you must do it. The severing of the old leaf is not the intended end. If it stops with that, the purpose is missed. We were created for more than our own spiritual development. Ultimately, the goal of maturity goes beyond development to reproduction—reproduction in others. A note of caution is here given lest one's interest becomes totally concentrated upon his own spiritual well-being to the neglect of the needy, hungry hearts nearby.

CONCLUSION

Spiritual truth is spiritually revealed. Every believer has the capacity to receive insight concerning this teaching. God has so designed us that truth feeds through the mind. It is the truth we *know* that sets us free. The Holy Spirit illumines the Word and makes it real to our hearts. Regardless of intellectual capacity, every Christian has the apparatus to perceive deep insight into spiritual mysteries.

After hundreds of hours of study, prayer, meditation and conversation on this subject, I have come to this settled conclusion. This is the heart of the Gospel. I was crucified with Christ. I was buried with Christ. I was resurrected with Christ. This must be acknowledged and accepted by faith. "Not I, but Christ" is meant to be the portion of *every* child of God.

THE GOSPEL

I Cor. 15:3-4		
JESUS CRUCIFIED	**BURIED**	**RESURRECTED**

Gal. 2:20		
CRUCIFIED WITH CHRIST	I LIVE, YET NOT I	CHRIST LIVES IN ME

Rom. 6:6	Rom. 6: 4-5	Rom. 6:4
OLD MAN CRUCIFIED	BAPTISM: PICTURE OF BURIAL	RESURRECTION LIFE

Col. 3:3	Col. 3:5	Col. 3:10
LIFE HID WITH CHRIST	MORTIFY YOUR MEMBERS	PUT ON NEW MAN

EXECUTION	TERMINATION	SUBSTITUTION

Rom. 6:6	Rom. 6:11	Rom. 6:16
KNOW	RECKON	YIELD

PRINCIPLE OF KNOWLEDGE	PRINCIPLE OF FAITH	PRINCIPLE OF TIME

MENTAL COMPREHENSION	VOLITIONAL ACCEPTANCE	EXPERIENTIAL VICTORY

TRUTH KNOWN TO US	TRUTH APPLIED BY US	TRUTH REAL IN US

TRUST THE WORD	RECKON BY FAITH	WALK IN SPIRIT

2 Cor. 5:14-15		
SIN (One died for all)	SELF (Not live unto themselves)	SPIRIT (but unto Him)

THE CROSS AND

CRUCIFIED

*SPHERE OF DEATH

Death passed upon all . . . all sinned	Rom. 5:12
Wages of sin is death	Rom. 6:23
Dead in trespasses and sin	Eph. 2:1

FIRST ADAM

First Adam, a living soul	I Cor. 15:45
First man, of the earth	I Cor. 15:47
Old man corrupt through deceitful lusts	Eph. 4:22
Put off old man with his deeds	Col. 3:9

DARKNESS

Walks in darkness, darkness blinded his eyes	I Jn. 2:11

CAPTIVITY

Walked . . . according to prince of power of air	Eph. 2:2
Satan has blinded minds of unbelievers	II Cor. 4:4

INDEPENDENCE

Alienated and enemies in your mind	Col. 1:21

THE FLESH

They of the flesh mind things of the flesh	Rom. 8:5
Fleshy mind is enmity against God	Rom. 8:7

BONDAGE

The spirit of bondage . . . unto fear	Rom. 8:15
Subject to bondage	Ga. 4:3

NATURAL

Carnal and walk after manner of men	I Cor. 3:3
Natural man receiveth not	I Cor. 2:14

UNBELIEF

Evil heart of unbelief	Heb. 3:12
Basic cause for lack of victory	Heb. 4:11
Whatsoever, not of faith is sin	Rom. 14:23

SPHERE OF SELF

Everyone saith, <u>I</u>	I Cor. 1:12
Trusted in themselves	Lu. 18:9
All seek their own	Phil. 2:21

*SPHERE: (realm or field of influence)

THE CHRISTIAN

H CHRIST

	SPHERE OF LIFE
Rom. 6:23	Free gift of God is eternal life
Rom. 8:2	Spirit makes free from sin and death
Rom. 5:17	Abundance of grace, reign in life
	SECOND ADAM
I Cor. 15:45	Last Adam . . . life giving spirit
I Cor. 15:47	Second man, of heaven
Eph. 4:24	New man is after God created in righteousness
Col. 3:10	Put on new man, renewed in knowledge
	LIGHT
I. Jn. 1:5	God is light and in Him is no darkness
	VICTORY
I Cor. 15:57	God gives the victory through Lord Jesus
Eph. 4:11	Able to stand against the Devil
	DEPENDENCE
Phil. 1:21	For me to live is Christ
	THE SPIRIT
Rom. 8:5	They of the spirit mind things of the spirit
Rom. 8:6	Mind of spirit is life and peace
	SONSHIP
Rom. 8:15	The spirit of adoption, Abba Father
I Pe. 1:14	Free in Christ to be obedient
	THE SUPERNATURAL
I. Cor. 2:12	Received the spirit which is of God
I. Pe. 4:6	Live according to God in the spirit
	FAITH
Ga. 3:24	Justified by faith
I. Jn. 5:4	Faith in God is the victory
Heb. 10:38	The just shall live by faith
	CHRIST
Gal. 2:20	No longer I, but Christ

THE TWO SIDES OF THE CROSS

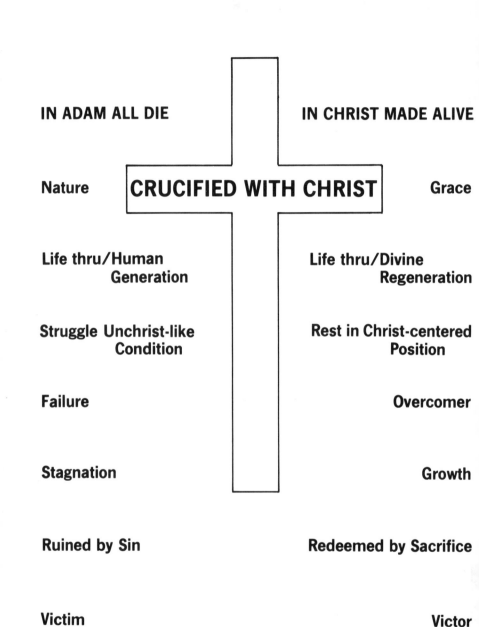

IN ADAM ALL DIE

IN CHRIST MADE ALIVE

Nature

CRUCIFIED WITH CHRIST

Grace

Life thru/Human
Generation

Life thru/Divine
Regeneration

Struggle Unchrist-like
Condition

Rest in Christ-centered
Position

Failure

Overcomer

Stagnation

Growth

Ruined by Sin

Redeemed by Sacrifice

Victim

Victor

UNION WITH CHRIST

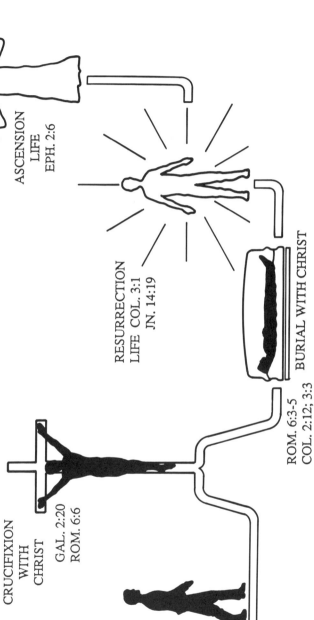

CRUCIFIXION
WITH
CHRIST

GAL. 2:20
ROM. 6:6

RESURRECTION
LIFE COL. 3:1
JN. 14:19

ASCENSION
LIFE
EPH. 2:6

BURIAL WITH CHRIST

ROM. 6:3-5
COL. 2:12; 3:3

Christ Life Ministries on the Internet!

Christ Life Ministries is committed to providing messages, material, and ministries that will further revival, both personally and corporately, in the local church.

- *Spiritual Life Crusades*
- *Prayer Advances*
- *Christ Life Publications*

Visit our web site to:
- Learn about the Prayer Advances for men, ladies, youth, and couples
- Sign up for our on-line newsletter
- Listen to over forty sermons from the Prayer Advances
- Review publications and resources that will help you and your family
- Learn more about Christ Life Ministries

www.christlifemin.org

New From Christ Life Publications!

TIME WITH GOD DEVOTIONAL DIARY

Would you like to read through the entire Bible in just one year? Are you interested in a tool that will assist you in organizing your Bible study? Do you desire to help your family develop the daily discipline of studying God's Word?

If you answered "Yes" to any of the above questions, then TIME WITH GOD is the answer. TIME WITH GOD provides you with a reasonable reading schedule that will get you through the Scripture in a single year. It also will assist you in contemplating the Word by furnishing space to record your thoughts each day.

Accountability is another great benefit when the entire family is working through the TIME WITH GOD diary. Whatever your age, you can begin studying to show yourself approved TODAY!

The attractive four color cover makes this spiral bound volume both appealing and practical. It has 206 numbered pages. ORDER YOURS TODAY!

Other Titles from Christ Life Publications

*FORGIVENESS: How To Get Along With Everybody All the Time! by Harold Vaughan and T.P. Johnston. "In a world filled with so much hatred and misunderstanding, few subjects are as timely as forgiveness. And yet, few works of biblical accuracy have been written on this important subject. Vaughan and Johnston's book is the best, purest and most practical treatment of the subject I know. Everyone who has been forgiven should read this book to know how and why to forgive."
 - Woodrow Kroll, Back to the Bible

*"Lord, Help Me Not To Have These EVIL THOUGHTS!" by Harold Vaughan. Quite often many Christians pray this prayer, but instead of thoughts ceasing, they only intensify. Here's a practical guide to achieving a healthy thought-life while engaged in mental warfare. This is no quick and easy method, but a divinely ordered plan of mental purity that has historically cleansed the most vile of minds.

*PRAYER SECRETS by Guy H. King. In a simple, direct, warm style Guy H. King uncovers these prayer secrets, one by one, from the Scriptures. The reader is treated to 26 tremendous chapters highlighted by headings and subheadings. Despite the depth of the subject matter, there is profound, challenging, encouraging, and convicting truth in these pages.

*The NATURE of a GOD-SENT REVIVAL by Duncan Campbell. Will it be business as usual or the usual business of revival? This powerful booklet is packed with power from a man who saw spiritual awakening in his ministry. Thousands were converted when God stepped down from Heaven in the Hebrides.

*View our latest resources at: www.christlifemin.org

ORDER FORM

Quantity Prices (U.S. Funds)

What It Means to Be CRUCIFIED With CHRIST
Prices subject to change

1-4 copies $4.00 each
5-10 copies $3.50 each
11-24 copies $3.00 each
25-49 copies $2.50 each
50-99 copies $2.00 each
100 or more copies $1.75 each

Quantity

_____ What It Means to Be CRUCIFIED With CHRIST

_____ Time With God Diary $10.95

_____ FORGIVENESS: How To Get Along With
          Everybody All the Time! $7.95

_____ "Lord, Help Me Not To Have These EVIL THOUGHTS!" $4.99

_____ Prayer Secrets $6.95

_____ The Nature of a God-Sent Revival $3.00

Shipping and handling (U.S. rates):
Under $25.00 add $4.00
$25.01 - $40.00 add $5.00
$40.01 - $50.00 add $6.00
$50.01 - $75.00 add $7.00
Over $75.00 add 9%

VA residents add 4 1/2% Sales tax

TOTAL $ _____

Make checks payable to:
CHRIST LIFE PUBLICATIONS
P.O. BOX 399, Vinton, VA 24179

NAME: _____

ADDRESS: _____

CITY: _____ STATE: _____ ZIP: _____

Credit card orders phone (540) 890-6100
**View all our resources at: www.christlifemin.org*